The Adventures of Blind Tom

Obiora N. Anekwe

The Adventures of Blind Tom
All Rights Reserved.
Copyright © 2015 Obiora N. Anekwe
v3.0

Cover Photo © 2015 Obiora N. Anekwe

Ethically Speaking Press

ISBN: 978-0-578-16481-6

Library of Congress Control Number: 2015943147

PRINTED IN THE UNITED STATES OF AMERICA

For our unborn child, who is loved even before birth.

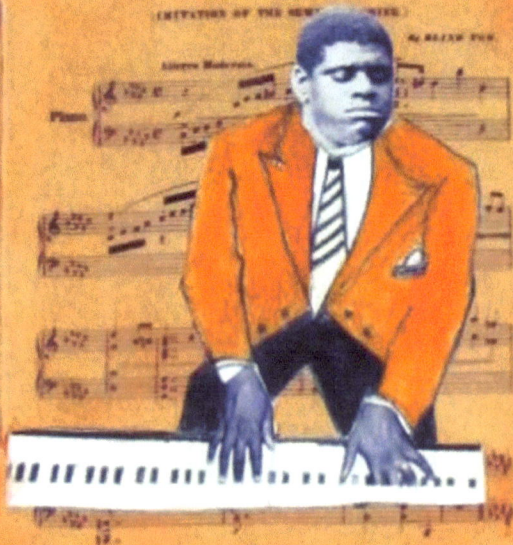

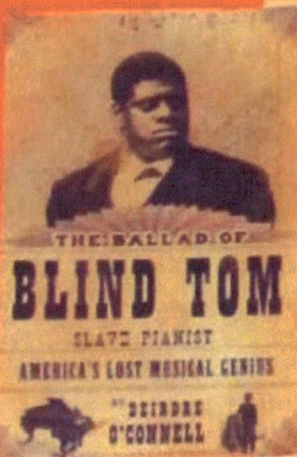

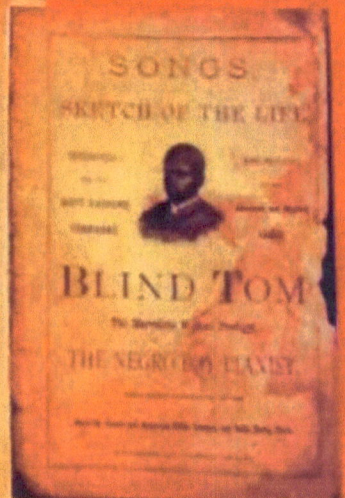

Thomas Wiggins was his name.

Nicknamed Blind Tom people would say

For he was blind and could play

That big old piano at night without a trace.

Ahiora N. Anakwe
4-29-2015
"Make a Joyful
Noise!"

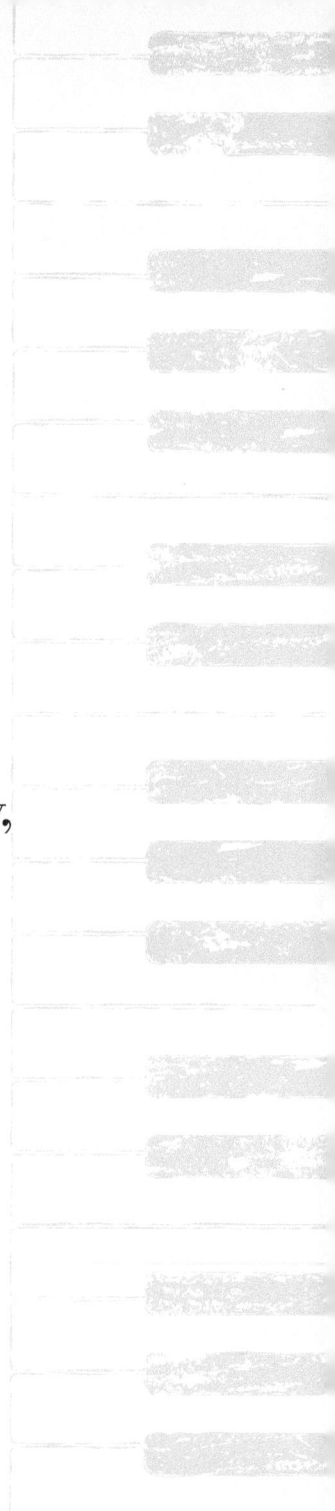

One night his master, Master Bethune, heard him play,

Thinking it was his daughter.

"Blind Tom, how could you play?"

Gloria R. Archives
5-7-2015
"Music on My Mind"

He could not see, but he could hear

Any song, a sound, and play it back in his own little way.

He could hear the winds. And play it back in his way.

He could hear the river. And play it back in his own little way.

He could hear the lightening. And play it back in his way.

Any sound he could hear. And play it back in his own little way.

Little Blind Tom loved to hear tiny sounds

Sound of winds spinning through mid air.

He dreamed of music throughout each night.

Unlike anyone else,

Music was a gift he wanted to share.

He was only nine of age

When many folks would say,

"This boy sure knows he can play!"

They said it was his songs that made him sway.

In every manner, in every kind of way.

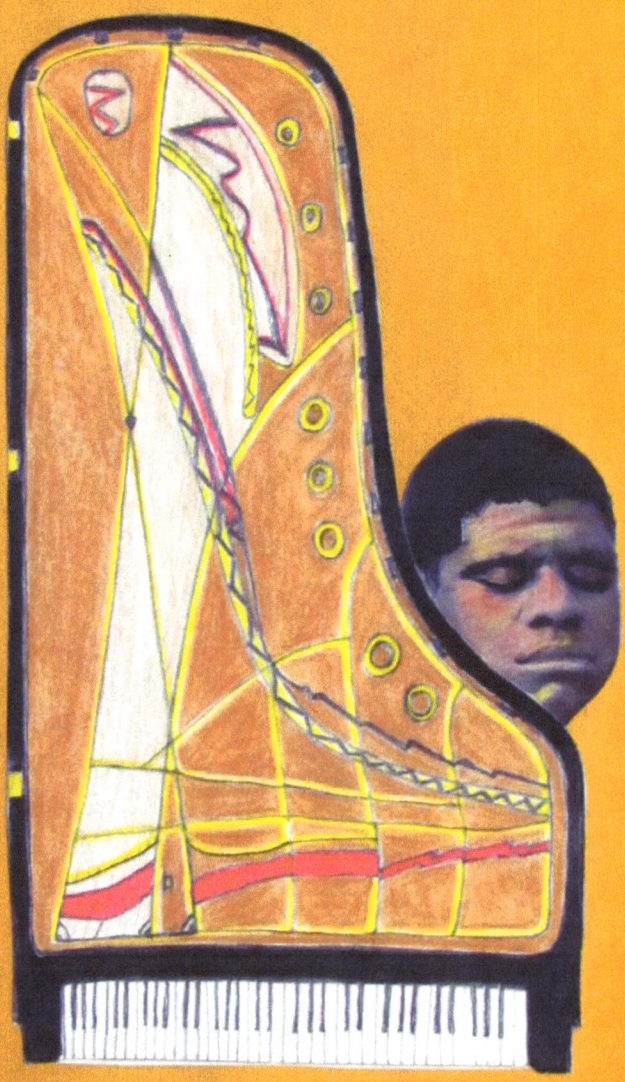

Oline N. Anakwe
4/7/2015
"The Original Piano Man"

He could play so well,

His music would put you in a spell.

Blind Tom was the Original Piano Man,

Able to play even with just one hand!

Olivia N. Anekwe
3/21/2015
"Wind Tom plays the piano at
the White House!"

Women and men from near and far would come to

Hear him play like a star.

He played for famous people like Mark Twain,

For royalty,

Even President Buchanan at the White House.

Obiora N. Anekwe
4-18-2015
"Leap for Joy!"

Blind Tom would leap for joy.

Ever so coy

Once an audience clapped for more!

Bigger and bigger he became,

And better and better he would play.

Blind Tom was his name

Many would say.

The tales of Blind Tom

Continue until today.

He will be known

As the boy who became

The man who could play a note

In any kind of way.

The End.

Afterword

Thomas "Blind Tom" Wiggins (1849-1908) was born in Harris County, Georgia and reared as a slave in Columbus, Georgia. He was a blind, autistic savant classical pianist, singer, and composer who became one of the nineteenth century's most extraordinary musical performers and composers. His stage name was Blind Tom. He traveled around the world, with the companionship of his slave master, entertaining audiences of people who spoke different languages from various other cultures. When he would perform, Blind Tom would introduce himself in the third person. He often learned the language of each country he visited in order to greet his audiences

in their native languages. Blind Tom became so famous that he earned around $100,000 annually during the mid 1800s. Known as the first African American to perform as an entertainer at the White House under the U.S. presidency of James Buchanan, Blind Tom also performed for other famous people like writer Mark Twain. Blind Tom is remembered as the "Original Piano Man" who entertained audiences with his piano playing and singing before modern entertainers such as Elton John and Billy Joel began performing their music to audiences around the world.

Acknowledgments: Although all images were photographed and/or artistically created by the artist, the facial images of Thomas "Blind Tom" Wiggins were provided by the Library of Congress Prints and Photographs Division.

www.ingramcontent.com/pod-product-compliance
Lightning Source LLC
Chambersburg PA
CBHW042002100426
42813CB00019B/2956